FANTASTIC EATS!

& HOW TO COOK THEM

·

FOR OTTS, MR MAN
AND BEAR
X

For Gemma Thomas – the kindest, funniest and most amazing friend anyone could have asked for and, to top it all off, a brilliant cook. I miss sharing recipes with you and I know how much you wanted me to write this book. I hope you like it.

xxxxxxx

Publishing Director Sarah Lavelle
Editor Harriet Webster
Copy Editor Sally Somers
Designer Luke Bird
Photographer Ellis Parrinder
Food Stylist Tamara Vos
Props Stylist Charlie Phillips
Production Director Vincent Smith
Production Controller Tom Moore

Published in 2019 by Quadrille, an imprint of Hardie Grant Publishing

Quadrille
52–54 Southwark Street
London SE1 1UN
quadrille.com

Cataloguing in Publication Data: a catalogue record for this book is available from the British Library.

Text © Angellica Bell 2019
Photography © Ellis Parrinder 2019
Design © Quadrille 2019

ISBN 978 1 78713 273 3

Printed in China

FANTASTIC EATS!

& HOW TO COOK THEM

ANGELLICA BELL

PHOTOGRAPHY BY ELLIS PARRINDER

Hardie Grant

QUADRILLE

CONTENTS

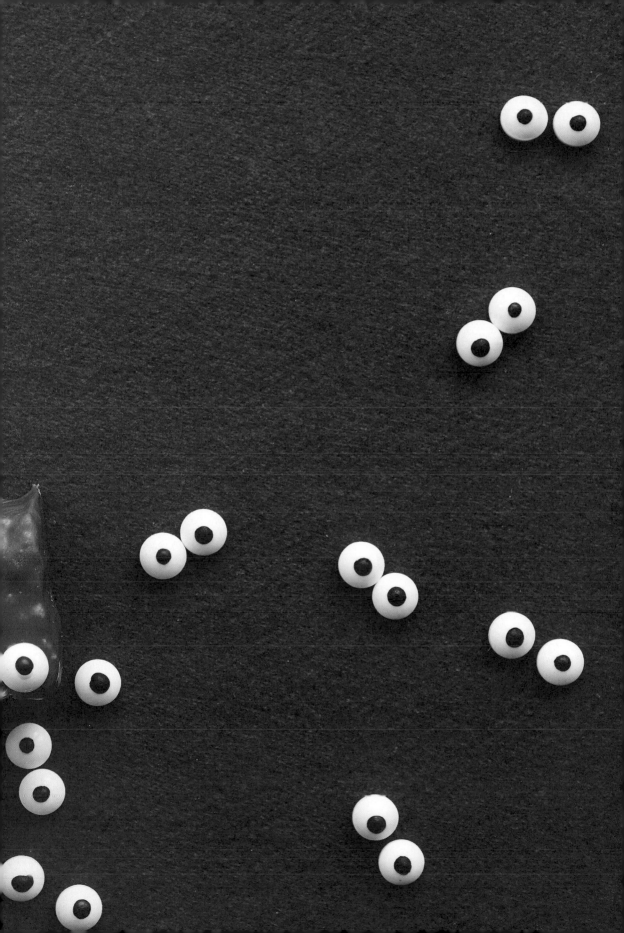

Hello and welcome to my first ever cookbook. Now, I need to make this clear from the start, I am not a trained chef (although it was one of the options on my list of things I wanted to be when I was a little girl, along with a police officer, teacher and lawyer!) – but I have always enjoyed eating food and cooking it. I think this appreciation started when I was a youngster hanging out with my grandmother in her kitchen. Her house was always so inviting; even before you walked through the door, you could smell her food wafting down the street, and you knew you'd be going home with your tummy full. She was a cook by trade but also loved home cooking, and would get me working in her kitchen descaling whole fish, baking cakes, cooking rice and preparing lots of West Indian food. But, don't panic, you'll only be doing some of those things in this book!

The point I'm trying to make is that my relationship with food started when I was very young – spending time in the kitchen and being able to learn through 'doing' meant that I grew up with a love for cooking, and now have the skills to serve up a plate of food of which I am really proud. That's why I thought a cookbook for children, young people and those who want to try some basic recipes, would be perfect. Within these pages I've shared a range of fantastic eats, along with some basic cooking techniques, to help you progress on your cooking journey. I'm not saying you will end up owning your own restaurant, or be awarded a Michelin star, but I believe that if you learn to cook and eat well, it will help to create some brilliant memories, whether at home with your family, when you've invited some friends over, or if you decide to take cooking beyond your childhood kitchen and into the world of adulthood. Some of the best times I've had were at the dinner table with my friends talking about silly stuff over a meal I've thrown together.

All I want is for you to be confident in the kitchen and have a go. Don't worry if it doesn't go right the first time, just try again. Lots of recipes went wrong when I first attempted them and it was so frustrating. I even remember once burning an apple crumble a few years ago when I had friends coming over… EMBARRASSING! It can happen to anyone!

Anyway, enough waffling from me. I just want to say thank you for buying my cookbook, and please enjoy making the recipes. Let me know how you get on or pop your pictures up on Instagram, tagging @fantasticeatscookbook.

X

BASICS

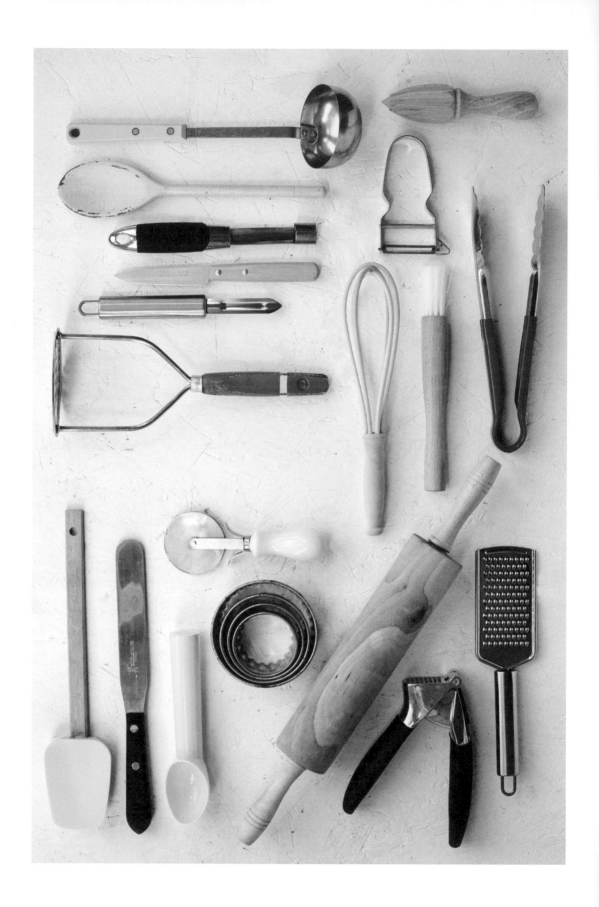

Blender

⚠ Blenders have very sharp blades, so ask an adult to help you when using one. Never put your hands inside the blender – use a spoon or spatula instead, and only when the blender is turned off. Always make sure the lid is fitted tightly before you turn it on.

Knife

⚠ Knives are very sharp, so always ask a grown-up before you use one – they can show you how to handle the knife properly and, when they think you are ready, let you try chopping something with supervision.

Grater

⚠ Always make sure your grater is standing on a stable surface and that you hold it by the handle at the top so that it doesn't topple over. Graters are very sharp so be very careful of your fingers.

Oven

⚠ Ovens get extremely hot so always ask a grown-up before you use one. Always wear oven gloves when taking things in and out of the oven and always remember to turn the oven off when you have finished cooking.

Grill

⚠ Grills get extremely hot very quickly, so always ask a grown-up before you use them. Always wear oven gloves when taking things out from under the grill and always remember to turn the grill off when you have finished cooking.

Food Processor

⚠ Food processors have very sharp blades, so ask an adult to help you when using one. Never put your hands inside the food processor – use a spoon or spatula instead, and only when it is turned off. Always make sure the lid is fitted tightly before you turn it on.

Stove

⚠ Whether you have an electric, induction or gas stove (sometimes called a hob), it will get very hot very quickly, so always keep your fingers away from the heat. If you have a gas stove there will be an open flame, so it's really important to have long hair tied back and remove long sleeves and scarves so that they don't dangle in the flame.

NOTE: Wash your hands with soap and warm water before you start cooking, and always after handling raw meat.

CHOPPING VEGETABLES

Whatever vegetable you are chopping, make sure you hold the veg steady with one hand.

With a sharp knife, gently push down on the vegetable where you want to cut.

Continue chopping, being very careful to keep your fingers out of the way.

Make sure you do this with a grown-up present because knives are very sharp!

CRUSHING GARLIC

Chop the ends off your garlic cloves and peel away the papery skin.

Pop your peeled cloves into a garlic crusher and squeeze really hard until your minced garlic appears.

(If you don't have a garlic crusher, don't worry, you can just cut your garlic cloves into really tiny pieces using a small knife.)

STONING AND PEELING AN AVOCADO

Using a knife, carefully cut all the way round the avocado until you hit the hard stone in the middle.

Hold both sides of the avocado and twist in opposite directions to pull it apart. You should have one half with the stone and one half without.

Press your knife into the stone and twist to remove (you might want to ask a grown-up to do this bit!).

Using a spoon, scoop out all the delicious pale green flesh.

GRATING GINGER

Take a small chunk of ginger and grate it, being very careful not to catch your fingers.

ZESTING CITRUS FRUITS

Hold a clean, unwaxed lemon or lime in one hand and a zester in the other.

Press down quite hard with the zester at the top of your lemon or lime and, still pressing hard, drag the zester down to the bottom of the fruit.

Repeat this all over your lemon or lime until it is completely zested.

(Ask a grown-up if you have a zester – if not, you can use a grater instead to remove the zest.)

JUICING CITRUS FRUITS

With a sharp knife, cut your lemon or lime in half.

If you have a lemon reamer or juicer, you can push this into the middle of your lemon or lime half and twist backward and forwards over a bowl until all the juice comes out.

If you don't have a reamer or juicer it's not a problem! Just take your lemon or lime half and squeeze it tightly over a bowl until all the juice comes out. Remember to pick out the pips!

CORING AN APPLE

Place an apple corer at the top of your apple over the stalk.

Holding the apple steady, carefully push down with the corer until it disappears into the apple. You might have to twist the corer or get a grown-up to help you if you can't push it down far enough.

Once you've reached the bottom of the apple, pull the corer back up to remove the apple core.

(If you don't have an apple corer you can cut the apple into quarters lengthways, then carefully cut out the core with a knife. Best to get a grown-up to help with this.)

PEELING AN APPLE

Hold an apple in one hand and a peeler in the other.

Press down quite hard with the peeler at the top of your apple and, still pressing, drag the peeler down to the bottom of the apple.

Repeat until you have completely peeled your apple.

(Once you get really good, see if you can peel the apple in a spiral all in one go!)

CRACKING EGGS

Tap an egg gently on the side of a bowl until you see the shell start to break.

Holding the egg above the bowl with both hands, gently push your thumbs into the cracked egg and pull the shell apart.

Your egg should plop into the bowl.

Remember to wash your hands afterwards.

SEPARATING EGGS

Begin with two clean bowls in front of you. Tap an egg gently on the side of one of the bowls until you see the shell start to break.

Holding the egg above one of the bowls with both hands, gently push your thumbs into the cracked egg and pull the shell apart a tiny bit – just enough so that the egg white starts leaking out into the bowl.

Very carefully, pull the shell apart, keeping the yolk in one half of the shell.

Gently tip the egg yolk onto your hand and let the rest of the egg white trickle through your fingers into the bowl.

Once all the white is gone, pop the egg yolk into the other bowl.

EGG WASHING

Crack an egg into a bowl (see page 17) and beat with a whisk or fork.

Dip a pastry brush into the beaten egg and paint it all over your pastry.

When the pastry is baked the egg will give it a lovely shine!

ROLLING PASTRY OR DOUGH

Sprinkle some flour onto a clean, dry work surface and place your pastry or dough on top.

Sprinkle your rolling pin with a little more flour.

Press down on the pastry or dough with the rolling pin and push away from you.

Keep pushing and rolling in lots of different directions until the pastry or dough is at the desired thickness.

SAVOURY

This easy recipe is a great way to try out the different flavours in my sweet and smoky BBQ sauce. It goes so well with the chicken and makes a tasty snack.

SERVES 4

Ingredients

8–10 chicken drumsticks
salt and black pepper
crusty baguettes, to serve

For the marinade
225g (¾ cup) tomato ketchup
60g (5 tablespoons) brown sugar
2 tablespoons Worcestershire sauce
1 tablespoon vinegar (such
    as apple cider vinegar or
    red wine vinegar)
1 tablespoon Dijon mustard
2 tablespoons smoked paprika
1 teaspoon garlic powder

For the coleslaw
½ red cabbage (you can use
    white if you want, or mix them)
2 carrots
3 spring onions (scallions)
2 tablespoons sultanas
    (golden raisins)
3 tablespoons low-fat mayonnaise
1 teaspoon Dijon mustard
1 teaspoon vinegar (such as
    apple cider vinegar or red
    wine vinegar)

1   To make the marinade, mix together the ketchup, sugar, Worcestershire sauce, vinegar, mustard, paprika and garlic powder in a large bowl.

2   Sprinkle salt and pepper over your chicken drumsticks, then add them to the marinade, making sure they are well coated all over. Cover the bowl with clingfilm and leave them to sit for at least 20 minutes in the refrigerator.

3   To make the coleslaw, place the cabbage cut side down on a chopping board and slice into fine shreds. Peel then grate the carrots on the large holes of a box grater (take care of your fingers). Trim the tops and bottoms off the spring onions and cut into small slices. Put the cabbage, carrots, spring onions and sultanas in a large bowl and stir until all the ingredients are mixed together.

4   Mix the mayonnaise with the mustard and vinegar with a spoon in smaller bowl. Give it a taste to check you're happy and add more salt and pepper if you need to. Pour this mixture over the cabbage and carrot mix then stir it all together. Place the coleslaw in the refrigerator for later.

5   Preheat the oven to 200°C/400°F/Gas mark 6 and pop a large piece of foil in a roasting tin.

6   Put the chicken drumsticks in the roasting tin with their sticky marinade. Roast for about 45 minutes, turning the chicken over halfway through the cooking time (set a timer as a reminder), with a large spoon or using tongs (get a grown-up to help you if you need to). The chicken needs to be cooked all the way through and be crispy on the outside. Take the tin out of the oven and let the drumsticks cool slightly before handling them.

7   Grab some bowls and spoon some coleslaw into each, then place a chicken drumstick or two on top. Serve with some crusty baguettes on the side.

BBQ
CHICKEN
COLESLAW

BIG
BEEFY
BURGERS

There are hundreds of ways to make a burger, but one thing's for sure, they always taste great when you make them at home. So, to ensure you rustle up the best juicy burgers, don't over-handle the meat, never flatten them with a spatula and only flip them once. I like to grill the meat because it's healthier.

SERVES 4

___

Ingredients

1 small red onion
500g (1lb 2oz) minced (ground) beef
2 tablespoons tomato ketchup
2 tablespoons English mustard
½ tablespoon Worcestershire sauce
½ teaspoon dried rosemary
½ teaspoon salt
1 teaspoon black pepper
4 slices of cheese
   (use your favourite)
4 burger buns

To serve

optional extra toppings: sliced tomato,
   lettuce, avocado, mayo and ketchup
oven chips (optional)
salad (optional)

1 Peel the red onion and finely chop it into small pieces. Place the onion in a large bowl with the beef, ketchup, mustard, Worcestershire sauce, rosemary, salt and pepper and mix everything together with a wooden spoon. Use your hands to form the mixture into 4 burger patties and gently flatten each one, trying not to squash or overwork the meat. Place the burgers on a baking tray and let them rest for 10 minutes at room temperature.

2 Preheat your grill to medium–hot (you don't want it too high). Place the baking tray with your burgers on under the grill and let them cook well on one side for at least 5 minutes. Carefully flip them over with a spatula and grill for another 4–5 minutes, until they are cooked through.

3 Meanwhile, gather all your extra toppings on the table, ready for everyone to get stuck into once the burgers are cooked.

4 When the burgers have 1 minute of cooking time left, lay a slice of cheese on top of each one and allow it to melt slightly before taking the burgers out from under the grill.

5 Slice your burger buns in half and toast the cut side under the grill – keep a close eye on them because they will brown very quickly!

6 At the table, place the burgers on the bun bases and start assembling your big beefy burger!

These are so delicious. I love the brightness of the fritters and the flavour combinations, and sometimes it's lovely to eat something that's simple but super tasty. It's also a great way to get vegetables into your diet!

SERVES 4

Ingredients

340g (2½ cups) grated
   butternut squash
340g (2½ cups) grated sweet
   potatoes
1 small onion
2 large eggs
90g (⅔ cup) plain (all-purpose) flour
¼ teaspoon baking powder
½ teaspoon garlic powder
½ teaspoon dried thyme
a few sage leaves, finely chopped
   (or 1 teaspoon dried sage)
pinch of grated nutmeg
½ teaspoon salt
pinch of black pepper
olive oil, for frying

To serve
sour cream
a few chives, finely chopped
fresh salad

1   Peel the squash, sweet potatoes and onion, then grate each of them using the large holes of a box grater – look after your fingers, you don't want to include them in the meal! Put the grated veg into a large bowl.

2   Break the eggs into a small bowl and whisk lightly with a fork (see page 17). Add them to the grated veg along with all the other ingredients, except the oil, and give everything a good mix with a wooden spoon. If the mixture is too runny (egg sizes can differ) just add a little bit more flour. You don't want the consistency to be too thick either – just right so that the fritters hold their shape in the frying pan.

3   Heat a drizzle of olive oil in a frying pan over a medium heat. Once the oil is hot, scoop about 3 tablespoons of the mixture per fritter into the pan and press it down gently with a spatula. Keep the heat moderate so the fritter cooks all the way through and oil doesn't splutter everywhere – please be careful! Let the fritter cook for about 2–3 minutes until it browns nicely. Using a spatula, carefully flip the fritter over to cook on the other side for another few minutes.

4   Pop some kitchen paper on a large plate then place the cooked fritter on top. Repeat the cooking process, adding more oil to the frying pan if it dries out, until all of your fritter mixture has been used.

5   Serve your squash and sweet potato fritters topped with a dollop of sour cream and some chopped chives, with a fresh salad.

BUTTERNUT SQUASH AND SWEET POTATO FRITTERS

CARIBBEAN CHICKEN CURRY WITH RICE AND PEAS

This recipe takes me back to my days growing up eating West Indian food. My gran would take me on the 207 bus all the way to Shepherd's Bush Market in London to buy 'provisions', then we'd travel all the way back home for her to cook up a feast. This is an easy version of a chicken curry with rice and peas for you to get a taste of the Caribbean (where they call kidney beans 'peas'). Don't be afraid to cook rice – the first few times I cooked rice when I was young, I burned the pan! So, don't worry, just follow my instructions and you'll do better than I did.

SERVES 4 – 6
(depending on portion sizes!)

Ingredients

1 onion
1 garlic clove
5cm (2 inch) piece of fresh ginger
1 red chilli (optional)
600g (1lb 5oz) skinless chicken
    breast fillets
2 tablespoons oil
1 tablespoon mild curry paste
1 x 400ml (14oz) can of
    coconut milk
1 large mango
small bunch of fresh coriander
    (cilantro)
salt and black pepper

(ingredients continued
on the next page)

1   Peel and chop the onion into thin slices. Peel and crush the garlic (see page 12). Then peel and grate the ginger (see page 14). If you're using the chilli, split it in half lengthways with a small knife and remove the seeds to make it less spicy, then cut it into tiny pieces. Chop the chicken into bite-sized pieces.

2   Grab a medium saucepan, add the oil and heat over a low heat. Add the onion, garlic, ginger and chilli (if using) and cook for about 5 minutes.

3   Now add the chicken to the saucepan and sprinkle with plenty of salt and pepper. Cook for 5–10 minutes, mixing with a wooden spoon, until the chicken no longer looks translucent and has browned slightly.

4   Add the curry paste to the saucepan and cook for 1 minute. Open the can of coconut milk, add it to the saucepan and turn the heat up to low–medium. Cook for 20 minutes, stirring often, until the curry reduces to a thicker mixture.

5   While your curry is simmering, get going with the rice and peas. Trim the tops and bottoms off the spring onions and cut them into small slices. Peel and crush the garlic. Open the can of kidney beans, tip them into a sieve and rinse with cold water. Place the kidney beans, rice, spring onions, garlic and thyme into a large saucepan. Open the can of coconut milk and add it to the saucepan, then fill the empty can with water and add that to the pan too. Sprinkle with plenty of salt and pepper, then stir well with a wooden spoon.

6   Bring to the boil, then turn the heat down to low, place a lid on the pan and leave it to cook for 20 minutes – but keep an eye on it! Once the liquid has been absorbed by the rice, it should be cooked – carefully taste it to check. When it's ready, turn off the heat and fluff up the rice with a fork.

For the rice and peas
2 spring onions (scallions)
1 garlic clove
1 x 400g (14oz) can of
   kidney beans
400g (2¼ cups) long grain rice
sprig of fresh thyme
1 x 400ml (14oz) can of
   coconut milk

7   Peel and cut the mango into small cubes using the hedgehog method: cut down either side of the mango stone so that you have two halves. Cut a criss cross pattern in the mango flesh using a small knife. Then push the mango halves inside out. You can now easily cut the mango cubes away from the skin (see photo). Add the mango cubes to the thickened curry. Finely chop the coriander and add 2 tablespoons to the curry. Cook the curry for a few more minutes, stirring with a wooden spoon, then turn off the heat.

8   Spoon some rice onto each plate, add some chicken curry, sprinkle with some coriander and *voilà*! Dinner is served!

These are so moreish, great for a quick snack and simple to make. If you're not a fan of bacon or rosemary, just leave them out. This recipe makes 12 twists, but if you have leftover pastry and bacon, try to roll out a few more!

MAKES 12

Ingredients

1 x 375g (13¼oz) packet of pre-rolled
   all-butter puff pastry
plain (all-purpose) flour, for dusting
100g (3½oz) mature Cheddar cheese
1 tablespoon English mustard
1 teaspoon dried rosemary
12 slices of streaky bacon
1 egg
black pepper

1   Pop a large piece of baking parchment on a baking tray.

2   Place your pastry on a lightly floured kitchen top or large wooden board with the longest edge facing you.

3   Grate the cheese on the large holes of a box grater. Spread the mustard all over the pastry with a spoon, then sprinkle the rosemary and the grated cheese all over. Using your fingers, lightly press the cheese into the pastry to help it to stick. Sprinkle with plenty of pepper to give it a little kick.

4   Place the slices of bacon in rows on top of the cheese, leaving a small gap in between each slice. Try to cover the whole of the pastry (this might mean some slices going in different directions, to fill any gaps).

5   Using a large knife, carefully cut the pastry in between each slice of bacon. Taking one strip at a time, hold the strip at both ends and gently twist it in opposite directions, to give 4 twists (like a curly straw) then pop on the baking tray. The first time I did this, I made a mess, so don't worry if they don't look good at first – after a few goes they'll be perfect!

6   Repeat with the rest of the strips, leaving plenty of space between each one on the tray – puff pastry puffs up and out!

7   Put the baking tray in the refrigerator to chill for 30 minutes while you preheat the oven to 200°C/400°F/Gas mark 6.

8   Break the egg into a small bowl and lightly beat with a fork (see page 17). Remove the twists from the refrigerator and brush them all with the beaten egg, using a pastry brush (see page 19).

9   Place the tray in the oven and bake your twists for about 25–30 minutes, or until the pastry has risen and is a nice golden-brown colour. Carefully remove the tray from the oven and let your twists cool down before you eat them!

CHEESE AND BACON TWISTS

CHICKEN QUESADILLAS

This Mexican-style meal is great for a light snack, or even dinner, when you could add some spicy rice to make it more substantial. Now, don't be put off by the chilli as you can make this as spicy as you like or even leave the chilli out altogether – you're the chef! I think this meal has lots of flavour but at the same time doesn't require too much work. All I ask is that you take care by the stove. Just take your time and lower the heat if you need to.

**SERVES 4
AS A SNACK**

———

Ingredients

500g (1lb 2oz) skinless chicken
    breast fillets
3 tablespoons chicken fry
    mix (most supermarkets
    will stock this)
½ teaspoon dried oregano
½ teaspoon dried cumin
½ teaspoon chilli powder (optional)
1 red (bell) pepper
4–5 spring onions (scallions)
2 tablespoons vegetable oil
20g (1½ tablespoons) butter
4 flour tortillas
250g (8¾oz) Cheddar cheese
salt and black pepper

To serve
sour cream
guacamole (see page 71
    for homemade)
tomato salsa (see page 71
    for homemade)

1   Chop your chicken into small chunks or strips. Place the chopped chicken in a large bowl and add the chicken fry mix, oregano, cumin and chilli (if you can handle a bit of spice), with a pinch each of salt and pepper. Mix everything together with a wooden spoon until the chicken is coated.

2   Cut the red pepper in half, remove the white membrane and seeds and cut it into small pieces or slices. Trim the tops and bottoms off the spring onions and cut them into small slices.

3   Place a big frying pan on the stove over a low heat and add the oil. If the heat is too high, the oil may splutter and can seriously burn, so just take your time. Add the chicken to the pan and fry for a few minutes, stirring the chicken with a wooden spoon so it cooks evenly. After a few minutes, add the diced or sliced pepper and then a few minutes later the spring onions. Keep frying until the chicken is cooked through and browned slightly (cut a piece open; it should be white all the way through), then turn off the heat.

4   Preheat your oven to 180°C/350°F/Gas mark 4 and pop a piece of foil on a large baking tray (or use 2 trays). Melt the butter in a small bowl in the microwave, or in a small saucepan over a low heat. Grab a tortilla. Using a pastry brush, brush one side of the tortilla with butter and place the buttered side down on the baking tray. Repeat with another tortilla and place it next to the first one (or on another tray).

5   Spoon the chicken mixture evenly onto both tortillas. Grate the cheese using a box grater, then sprinkle this over the top of the chicken mixture. Place another tortilla on top of each and brush the tops with more melted butter.

6   Cook in the oven for 15 minutes or until the tortillas are crispy and golden. Remove from the oven and let them cool a little before cutting into wedges. Serve with sour cream, guacamole and tomato salsa.

Pizza is one of my favourite foods. There's a little Italian restaurant down the road from our house which we love to go to as a family – Lino, the Italian owner, is from Naples and he always tells us stories about where he grew up. But we also like to cook pizza at home. We don't have a pizza oven, but we give it a good go and thoroughly enjoy hanging out as a family, getting messy and then sitting down to enjoy our own take on the classic, while imagining we are sitting in a little trattoria in Naples on holiday!

SERVES 4

Ingredients

For the dough
500g (3½ cups) strong white
    bread flour, plus extra for dusting
1 x 7g sachet (2 teaspoons) dried
    easy-bake yeast
3 tablespoons extra virgin olive oil,
    plus extra for greasing and drizzling
1½ teaspoons salt
1½ teaspoons caster (superfine) sugar
250ml (1 cup) warm water

For the tomato sauce
2 garlic cloves
3 tablespoons extra virgin olive oil
large handful of basil leaves, plus
    extra to serve
2 x 400g (14oz) cans of peeled
    plum tomatoes
1 teaspoon sugar
1 tablespoon dried oregano
1 teaspoon salt
½ teaspoon black pepper

(ingredients continued
on the next page)

1   Start by making the dough. Put your flour into a large bowl and use a spoon to make a well in the centre. Tip the yeast, olive oil, salt, sugar and water into the well and knead everything together in the bowl with your hands for about 10 minutes, until you have a nice smooth dough. Add a bit of extra flour to help bind your dough if it's a bit sticky.

2   Tip your dough onto a work surface, drizzle the bowl well with some olive oil and put the dough back in the bowl. Flip the dough over so it's lightly oiled on both sides. Cover the bowl with a tea towel and let the dough prove (this means double in size) in a warm place for at least 1–2 hours.

3   Now it's time to make your homemade pizza sauce! You can buy this at the supermarket, but it's great to make your own and that way you know what's in it. Peel and crush the garlic (see page 12). Heat the oil in a medium saucepan over a low heat then add the garlic and fry for 1 minute. Stir in the basil leaves, tomatoes and their juice, sugar and oregano, and cook for 5 minutes, stirring with a wooden spoon.

4   Turn off the heat and leave the mixture to cool for 10 minutes, then blitz with a hand-held or stand blender until the tomato sauce is smooth. Add the salt and pepper, give it a taste and leave it on the side for later.

5   Preheat your oven to 220°C/425°F/Gas mark 7.

6   Let's get back to the dough! After it has doubled in size, tip it onto a lightly floured work surface. Press it down with your hands to get rid of any bubbles. Divide it into 4 pieces if you're making little pizzas, or into 2 pieces for big ones. Using a rolling pin, roll each ball of dough into a flat circle about 1cm (½ inch) thick (see page 19) and put it on to a baking sheet (you may need to cook these one at a time).

PIZZA!
PIZZA!
PIZZA!

For the topping
250g (8¾oz) grated mozzarella

Extra topping ideas
sliced ham, sliced mushrooms, pineapple
chunks, sliced red onion, sliced
courgettes, sliced red (bell) peppers,
sweetcorn, grated Parmesan

7   Drizzle your dough with some olive oil, making sure the
edges are covered too.

8   Using a spoon, spread some of your tomato sauce onto the
dough, leaving a clear border around the edge for the crust.
Sprinkle the grated mozzarella on top, followed by your
favourite toppings (try not to overload them otherwise they
won't cook properly). Pop the pizzas into the oven for 7–10
minutes for the smaller size, or 10–15 for the larger, until the
cheese is melted and the crust has turned slightly golden.

9   Finish off with a sprinkling of basil leaves.

LAMB KOFTAS, HOUMOUS AND FLATBREADS

I had to put this recipe in the cookbook as it was one of the tests that John and Gregg set me while I was on *Celebrity MasterChef* in 2017. I had 10 minutes to make it and just about managed, but don't worry, you can have more time if you like! I remember walking out of the kitchen that day thinking that it's so easy to make tasty food from scratch given a short space of time. So, here's the recipe for you to try. I love this even though it brings back scary memories of having my food tasted on *Celebrity MasterChef*!

SERVES 4–6

___

Ingredients

Houmous (see page 70)

For the salad
½ cucumber
1 garlic clove
a few mint leaves
80g (2¾oz) pomegranate seeds
salt and pepper

For the flatbreads
200g (1½ cups) self-raising flour,
    plus extra for dusting
¼ teaspoon baking powder
¼ teaspoon salt
200g (scant 1 cup) plain yogurt
small bunch of flat-leaf parsley
1 garlic clove
40g (3 tablespoons) butter

(ingredients continued
on the next page)

1 There are a few elements to this dish, so we can just take our time to get it all together. Begin with the salad. Chop the cucumber into small chunks and put them into a large bowl. Peel and crush the garlic (see page 12) and finely chop the mint, then add these to the bowl along with the pomegranate seeds. Sprinkle with a pinch each of salt and pepper and then mix everything together with a spoon.

2 Flatbreads are so easy to make you'll be surprised! In a large bowl, mix together the flour, baking powder, salt and yogurt with a wooden spoon to form a dough. Knead the dough in the bowl with your hands for 1 minute, then leave in the bowl to rest for 20 minutes.

3 Right, let's get our hands even more dirty with the koftas! In a large bowl, throw in the lamb, salt and pepper. Peel and crush the garlic, zest the lemon (see page 14) and add this to the lamb with the ras-el-hanout and the mango chutney. Give everything a good squeeze and mix with your hands! Divide the mixture into 8–10 portions and shape each one into long sausages around the skewers. Try to make them evenly-shaped and not too fat because you want them to cook all the way through. Drizzle each kofta with a little oil on both sides, then place on a baking tray (I put foil on my tray to save washing it later!).

4 Preheat the grill to medium. Place your koftas under the grill and cook for about 10–12 minutes, turning them regularly with tongs – keep an eye on them! Once browned and cooked through, take them out from under the grill and let them rest for a couple of minutes.

For the koftas
500g (1lb 2oz) minced (ground)
    lamb (20% fat)
½ teaspoon salt
1 teaspoon black pepper
1 garlic clove
zest of 1 lemon (see page 14)
1 tablespoon ras-el-hanout (you can
    buy this in any good supermarket)
4 tablespoons mango chutney
olive oil, for brushing

You will need 8–10 wooden
skewers, soaked in cold water

5   Back to the flatbreads. Divide the dough into four pieces
    and, using a rolling pin, roll each piece out on a lightly floured
    surface into, well, any shape you like (see page 19)! Round,
    oblong, wonky... whatever!

6   Grab a frying pan, or a ridged griddle pan if you have one,
    and heat it over a medium heat. Cook the flatbreads in the
    hot, dry pan one at a time for about a minute or so on each
    side until golden and slightly puffed (use tongs or a spatula to
    flip it over). Place the cooked flatbreads on a plate, keeping
    them warm by covering them with a tea towel.

7   Roughly chop the parsley and peel and crush the garlic.
    Melt the butter in a small bowl in the microwave, or in a
    small saucepan over a low heat. Add the parsley and garlic
    to the melted butter and mix with a spoon. Using a pastry
    brush, brush the garlic butter over each flatbread.

8   Grab your serving plates and place a flatbread, a couple of
    lamb koftas and some salad on each. Place the houmous in
    the centre of the table. You can now enjoy some flavours of
    the Middle East!

Here's a small twist on a big favourite. Made in a muffin tin for ease, you'll be producing a lovely Sunday lunch for the whole family. Serve these with mashed potatoes and vegetables and everyone will have a smile on their face.

SERVES 4 – 6

———

Ingredients

12 chipolata sausages
sunflower oil, for drizzling
150g (1 cup plus 2 tablespoons)
    plain (all-purpose) flour
3 eggs
150ml (10 tablespoons) milk
12 small sprigs of rosemary
salt and black pepper

1   First things first, preheat your oven to 220°C/425°F/ Gas mark 7.

2   If your chipolatas are attached to each other, snip them apart with scissors. Put a sausage in each of your muffin tin holes and drizzle them all with some oil. Place the tin in the oven for about 7 minutes, until the tops of the sausages are brown, then use a fork to turn them over and return to the oven for another 7 minutes so the underside can also brown.

3   While the sausages are cooking you can whip up the batter. Pop the flour in a large bowl, break in the eggs (see page 17) and whisk them using a balloon whisk. Slowly add the milk, whisking it in until you have a smooth batter. Sprinkle with a pinch each of salt and pepper. Now pour the batter into a jug to make it easier to pour into the holes of the baking tin.

4   Remove the sausages from the oven and place the tin on a heatproof surface – the oil and sausages will be very hot so use oven gloves and take care. Slowly and carefully pour batter over each of the sausages and throw a sprig of rosemary into each hole.

5   With a steady hand (or with some grown-up help!) place the tin back into the oven and cook for 15–20 minutes or until the batter is golden, puffed up and crispy.

6   Remove from the oven and let your little-toads-in-the-holes cool for a minute before carefully tipping them out of the tin.

LITTLE
TOADS IN
THE HOLES

MAC HAM
AND
CHEESE

Growing up, macaroni cheese was one of my favourite dishes to eat. This recipe will teach you to make a 'roux' (a base for a sauce using flour and butter), something that all chefs learn. When you add the flour to the melted butter, you may think something has gone wrong when you see the gloop form at the bottom of the pan, but just keep whisking and be confident! This is a lovely family meal that I like to serve with plenty of vegetables. If there are lots of you or you're really hungry, just double the ingredients listed below.

SERVES 4

Ingredients

175g (6¼oz) dried macaroni
20g (1½ tablespoons) butter
20g (2⅓ tablespoons) plain
   (all-purpose) flour
350ml (1½ cups) milk
1 teaspoon English mustard
100g (generous 1 packed cup) grated
   cheese (strong Cheddar tastes great,
   but you can use your favourite)
4 slices of ham
4 tablespoons dried white
   breadcrumbs (use golden if that's
   what you've got in the cupboard)
½ teaspoon dried thyme
½ teaspoon dried oregano
salt and black pepper

1   Preheat your oven to 180°C/350°F/Gas mark 4.

2   Place a large saucepan of water over a medium heat. When it is boiling, add a pinch of salt and the macaroni, then cook until the pasta has a slight 'bite' to it, otherwise known as 'al dente' (this will take 10 minutes). Tip into a colander to drain.

3   While your macaroni is cooking, let's make the sauce. Melt the butter in a medium saucepan over a low heat then add the flour, stirring continuously with a balloon whisk or wooden spoon. Mix to a smooth paste and keep stirring for a minute or so to cook the flour.

4   Keeping the heat low, start adding the milk little by little and whisking/stirring constantly. As the milk is added you will start to see it form a lovely sauce, thickening up after each addition. Once you've added all the milk, increase the heat to medium, add the mustard and stir until the sauce starts to bubble. Remove the sauce from the heat. Sprinkle with salt and pepper and add most of the cheese, keeping 4 tablespoons aside for the top. Stir the sauce until the cheese has melted.

5   Tip the drained macaroni into the sauce. Roughly chop the ham into small pieces and add this to the sauce too. Mix everything together then tip the mixture into an ovenproof dish, about 20cm (8 inches) in diameter.

6   In a medium bowl, mix together the breadcrumbs, dried herbs and remaining cheese with a spoon. Sprinkle this all over the cheesy macaroni then pop it in the oven for about 25 minutes, until golden and bubbling.

This is a fun way of making an omelette. You can mix different flavour combinations using your favourite ingredients, giving you some chef creativity (I've given you some suggestions in the ingredients list). I've kept this vegetarian, but feel free to add some ham or leftover cooked chicken (just use up anything available in the refrigerator!). These fun little individual omelettes are perfect for breakfast, lunch or a snack on-the-go! Just be careful lifting the muffin tin in and out of the hot oven, and always wear your oven gloves.

MAKES 12

Ingredients

olive oil, for greasing
1 small onion
150g (1¼ cups) frozen peas (you
    can also add chopped spinach,
    mini tomatoes or finely chopped
    mushrooms)
120g (1¼ cups) grated Cheddar
    cheese (or your favourite cheese)
1 teaspoon dried mixed herbs
6 large eggs
4 tablespoons milk
salt and black pepper

1   Preheat your oven to 180°C/350°F/Gas mark 4.

2   Drizzle some olive oil into each hole of your muffin tin and rub it around with your fingers until all the sides are well coated – this will stop your omelettes from sticking.

3   Peel and finely chop the onion into little pieces, then divide it equally between the muffin holes. Place the tin in the oven for 5 minutes.

4   Meanwhile, put your peas and cheese (and any other ingredients you've chosen) into a medium bowl, then add the dried herbs and mix with a wooden spoon.

5   Crack your eggs into a small bowl (see page 17), beat with a fork, then pour over the vegetables and cheese, stirring everything to make sure the peas separate. Add the milk, plus a pinch each of salt and pepper, then mix again.

6   Carefully take the muffin tin out of the oven.

7   Use a ladle to pour your omelette mixture into the 12 holes, then use a teaspoon to mix the contents of each hole.

8   Pop the tray back into the oven for 15–20 minutes until the omelette bites are cooked through and just turning golden. Let your omelette bites cool in the tin for a couple of minutes before scooping them out and serving.

OMELETTE
BITES

POPCORN CHICKEN & PARMESAN WEDGES WITH GARLIC SAUCE

Here's my take on chicken and chips for all of you out there who love it too.
I know you're probably wondering why on earth popcorn would go with
chicken, but trust me, it does, and I love the taste. See what you think!

SERVES 4

Ingredients

For the potato wedges
4 large potatoes, washed
4 tablespoons olive oil
1 teaspoon paprika
40g (½ cup) grated Parmesan cheese
large handful of parsley
salt and black pepper

For the popcorn chicken
50g (7–8 cups) cooked
    salted popcorn
50g (scant ½ cup) golden
    breadcrumbs
1 teaspoon dried thyme
salt and black pepper
2 eggs
50g (6 tablespoons) plain
    (all-purpose) flour
400g (14oz) skinless chicken
    breast fillets
100ml (generous ⅓ cup) vegetable oil

For the garlic sauce
3 garlic cloves
75g (⅓ cup) butter
200g (generous ¾ cup) crème fraîche
salt and black pepper

1   Preheat the oven to 200°C/400°F/Gas mark 6 and pop
    a piece of baking parchment on a baking tray.

2   Using a sharp knife, cut your potatoes in half lengthways.
    Cut the halves in half again lengthways, then the quarters
    in half till you have 8 pieces. Try to make them all the same
    size so they cook at the same rate.

3   In a large bowl, mix together the olive oil, paprika and some
    salt and pepper with a wooden spoon. Toss all the potato
    wedges in the mixture until they are coated. Place them on
    the baking tray, skin side down in a single layer, then sprinkle
    with half of the grated Parmesan and a little more salt. Bake
    in the oven for 35 minutes, until cooked through and golden.

4   While the wedges are cooking, let's get going with our
    popcorn chicken. Put the popcorn in a food processor and
    pulse until you have small crumbs. Tip the popcorn crumbs
    into a medium bowl and add the breadcrumbs, thyme, and
    a pinch each of salt and pepper. Give it a good mix.

5   In another medium bowl, crack your eggs (see page 17) and
    beat with a fork until well mixed.

6   Add the flour and a pinch of salt to another medium bowl.

7   Carefully cut the chicken into medium-sized strips and make
    sure the strips are properly dry – pat with kitchen paper if
    you need to. Dip one of the chicken strips first in the bowl
    of flour, then shake off any excess. Next dip the strip in the
    beaten egg, then finally in the popcorn mixture and then
    place on a large plate. Repeat these steps until you have
    coated all the chicken strips.

8   Heat the oil in a large frying pan over a medium heat and fry the strips, turning them with tongs a couple of times, until golden (they don't need to cook right through at this stage). Pop a piece of baking parchment on a baking tray and place the chicken strips on here once they are fried.

9   Your potato wedges should now be ready, so take them out of the oven carefully. Turn the oven temperature down to 180°C/350°F/Gas mark 4 and pop your chicken in the oven to bake for 8 minutes – keep an eye on it or set a timer.

10   While the chicken is baking, finely chop the parsley. Take the wedges off the tray with a spatula or tongs and pop them onto a serving plate. Sprinkle with the remaining Parmesan and half of the parsley.

11   To make the garlic sauce, melt the butter in a small saucepan over a medium heat. Peel and finely chop the garlic (see page 12), then add it to the saucepan and cook for 1 minute until softened. Turn the heat down to low, stir in the crème fraîche and the rest of the parsley, and sprinkle with a pinch each of salt and pepper. Your garlic sauce is ready.

12   By now the chicken should be cooked so carefully remove it from the oven using oven gloves.

13   Grab some serving plates. If you have tiny pots for the garlic sauce, put some in each and place on the plates. Add some wedges to each plate, then the chicken and a little fresh salad, if you like. All that's left to do is call those waiting for dinner to come and eat!

SHEPHERD'S PIE

This is a classic dish that everyone will love. Perfect if your friends are coming over after school, or as a nice winter treat to warm you up. This is a great recipe to have up your sleeve and you'll be making it even when you're a grown-up! It also tastes delicious the next day.

SERVES 4

————

Ingredients

3 large carrots
1 large onion
4 sprigs of fresh thyme
2 teaspoons fresh rosemary leaves,
    or 1 teaspoon dried
2 tablespoons olive oil
500g (1lb 2oz) minced (ground) lamb
2 tablespoons butter
125g (1 cup) frozen peas
2 tablespoons flour
2 tablespoons tomato paste
2 tablespoons Worcestershire sauce
1 tablespoon red wine vinegar
250ml (1 cup) chicken stock
salt and black pepper

For the mashed potato topping
6 large potatoes
4–5 tablespoons milk
2 tablespoons butter
1 egg

vegetables and crusty
    bread, to serve

1 Pop your oven on to 200°C/400°F/Gas mark 6.

2 Peel and finely chop the carrots. You want them to cook through, so make sure the pieces are small. Peel and finely chop the onion. Remove the thick thyme and rosemary stems and roughly chop the herbs.

3 Grab yourself a large, heavy saucepan and heat the oil over a medium heat. Add the carrots and cook, stirring with a wooden spoon, until they start to soften. Add the onion and keep cooking for another 2 minutes.

4 Add the lamb to the pan and keep cooking until all the meat goes from pink to brown, breaking it down with your wooden spoon to make sure there are no big lumps. Sprinkle with plenty of salt and pepper and add the rosemary and thyme. Once the meat is completely browned, turn off the heat.

5 The next thing to do is to drain away the meat fat. You'll need a sieve placed over a bowl, and maybe some grown-up help if your pan is heavy. Tip the meat mixture into the sieve and let the fat drain into the bowl underneath.

6 Put the meat mixture back into the pan and return it to a medium heat. Add the butter, peas and flour and stir with your wooden spoon.

7 Next, add the tomato paste, Worcestershire sauce, vinegar and stock. Stir, then let everything cook for about 15 minutes, until the liquid has become a lovely, thick, meaty gravy.

8 While the meat mixture is cooking, let's make the mashed potato. Peel all your potatoes, cut them into small pieces and put them into a large saucepan covered with cold water. Sprinkle with a pinch of salt, bring the water to the boil over a medium heat, then lower the heat and let the potatoes cook through. Prick the potatoes with a fork after 15–20 minutes to see if they are cooked: if not leave them a bit longer. When they feel soft, carefully tip the potatoes into a colander over the sink to drain. Leave them in the colander until they have stopped steaming.

9 Meanwhile, heat the milk in a small saucepan over a medium heat until just warm (you can also use a microwave). Melt the butter in a small bowl in the same way. Using a pastry brush, brush some of the butter inside a deep ovenproof dish that is big enough to hold all the meat and the potato.

10 Put the potatoes in a large bowl or back in the saucepan and start to mash them with a masher. Add the warm milk a little at a time until you get a nice smooth consistency, then add the rest of the melted butter and sprinkle with salt and pepper. Mash again to mix everything together.

11 Carefully spoon the meat mixture into the ovenproof dish, then spoon over your mashed potato and even out the top with the back of a spoon or a fork. Crack the egg into a small bowl (see page 17) and lightly beat with a fork. Using a pastry brush, brush the potato with the beaten egg. Pop it in the oven for about 20 minutes or until the potato is golden brown (you may even see some of the sauce bubbling round the sides). Take it out of the oven and let it rest for a while.

12 Set the table and call everyone round to start eating! Serve with your favourite vegetables and crusty bread.

This salmon dish has delicious Asian-inspired flavours for you to enjoy. I have loved eating fish from a young age, which has encouraged me to find interesting and easy ways to cook it. Served with brown rice or soba noodles, it's both healthy and tasty. I love it and hope you do too!

MAKES 12

Ingredients

3 garlic cloves
1 small piece of fresh root ginger (or use a pinch of ground ginger if you don't have fresh)
6 tablespoons low-salt soy sauce
5 tablespoons clear honey
2 tablespoons rice vinegar
1½ teaspoons sesame oil
4 x 100g (3½oz) skinless, boneless salmon fillets
2 carrots
1 small broccoli head
200g (7oz) baby sweetcorn
1–2 tablespoons sunflower oil, plus extra for greasing
a few spring onions (scallions)
sprinkling of sesame seeds
salt and black pepper

1   Firstly, make the marinade for the salmon. Peel and crush the garlic (see page 12) and grate the ginger (see page 14). In a small bowl, mix together the soy sauce, honey, rice vinegar, sesame oil, garlic and ginger with a spoon. Now place your four pieces of salmon into a dish so that they are tightly packed together. Sprinkle the salmon with a pinch each of salt and pepper on both sides and pour the marinade over the top. Cover with clingfilm and pop the dish in the refrigerator.

2   Now it's time to prepare your vegetables! Peel the carrots and slice them into thin rounds. Cut the broccoli into small pieces. Pop the sweetcorn, carrots and broccoli into a large bowl, drizzle over some sunflower oil and mix with a spoon.

3   Cut out four squares of foil, each about 30 x 30cm (12 x 12 inch), and drizzle each piece with oil right up to the edges.

4   Preheat your oven to 200°C/400°F/Gas mark 6 and grab a baking tray.

5   Time to fill your parcels. Place a quarter of the veg in the centre of each of your foil pieces then fold the sides up ready for the fish, so the marinade won't escape.

6   Grab the salmon fillets from the refrigerator and place a piece of fish on top of each of the vegetable piles. Spoon the leftover marinade over each piece of fish until it is used up.

7   Fold the edges of the foil over together to close your parcels and place them on your baking tray. Slide the tray into the oven and cook for 20 minutes. While they are in the oven, trim the tops and bottoms off the spring onions and cut them into small slices. Pop the spring onions in a bowl ready for serving.

8   Take the parcels out of the oven and let them rest for a few minutes while you get your serving plates out and set the table.

9   Place each parcel on a plate, open them up carefully, sprinkle each with some sesame seeds and spring onions and serve.

TERIYAKI SALMON PARCELS

TUNA AND SWEETCORN PASTA BAKE

I've been making this recipe since I was a child. I still make it today for friends when they come over, and for my little ones' parties too. Quite frankly, there is nothing wrong with enjoying canned food, especially when there's no time! As you get older, you can add your own personal touches to this recipe and use up what you have in the refrigerator – sautéed mushrooms, sautéed onions, peas... any vegetable really. Personally, I don't think I will ever stop eating this!

SERVES 8

_____

Ingredients

400g (14oz) your favourite pasta
    (I like spirali)
1 x 294g (10¾oz) can of Campbell's
    condensed cream of mushroom soup
a little milk
1 x 325g (12oz) can of sweetcorn
2 x 120g (4oz) cans of tuna in
    spring water
1 tablespoon dried mixed herbs
1 tablespoon olive oil
150g (5¼oz) Cheddar cheese
broccoli and carrots, to serve

1   Preheat your oven to 200°C/400°F/Gas mark 6. Place a large saucepan of water over a medium heat. When the water is boiling add a pinch of salt and your pasta.

2   While the pasta is cooking, grab the can of soup, open it and tip the contents into another large saucepan. Fill the empty can with milk and add it to the pan with the soup. Heat the soup and milk over a low heat, stirring with a wooden spoon until they are mixed together.

3   Open the can of sweetcorn and drain the liquid down the sink, then add the corn to the soup. Repeat with the cans of tuna and then add the mixed herbs. (If you are adding other ingredients, throw them in now!)

4   Once the pasta has a slight 'bite' to it, otherwise known as '*al dente*', tip it into a colander over the sink to drain. Put the pasta back in the saucepan and stir in the olive oil.

5   Pour the soup mixture into the pasta pot and give it a good mix. You may not need to add all the soup mixture – you don't want the mix too dry or too wet, but it depends on how you like it.

6   Tip the creamy pasta into a deep, large ovenproof dish about 26cm (10½ inches) in diameter. Then grate the cheese over the top using the coarse side of a box grater.

7   Pop the dish in the oven and bake for 25–30 minutes, until the cheese has melted and is bubbling and slightly golden. Carefully take it out of the oven and let it rest for 15 minutes before serving. I like to eat this with broccoli and carrots!

Baked beans are always popular, whether they're on toast, in jacket potatoes with cheese melted over the top, or stirred into some pasta (it's all I could afford at university!). Here's a recipe for you to make your own. Don't get me wrong, I love the beans out of a can, but these taste so good and you can adjust the salt and sugar. If you want to make a big pan, just double or triple the ingredients – you'll just need to do a bit of maths, which I'm sure you can handle!

SERVES 4
AS A SIDE

———————

Ingredients

½ onion
1 garlic clove
1 tablespoon vegetable oil
1 tablespoon tomato paste
½ teaspoon paprika
¼ teaspoon dried thyme
1 tablespoon brown sugar
1 tablespoon soy sauce
pinch of ground cloves
   (optional)
1 x 400g (14oz) can of
   cannellini beans
150g (⅔ cup) tomato passata
salt and black pepper

1 Right, let's get cooking your baked beans! Peel and finely chop the onion half. Peel and crush the garlic (see page 12). Heat the vegetable oil in a medium saucepan over a medium heat and add the onion and garlic. Cook for about 5 minutes until nice and soft.

2 Now add the tomato paste, paprika, thyme, sugar, soy sauce and cloves (if using). Give the mixture a good stir with a wooden spoon and cook for a couple more minutes.

3 Open the can of beans and tip the contents into a sieve over the sink. Run cold water through the beans to rinse. Add the beans and the tomato passata to the pan as well, then cook for at least 5 minutes, until the mixture is piping hot and the sauce has thickened a little. Sprinkle with a pinch of black pepper – you probably won't need salt because soy sauce is very salty, but add it if you think it needs it!

4 Last but not least, enjoy your baked beans whichever way you want!

HOMEMADE BAKED BEANS

USEFUL DIPS

SERVES 4 – 6

Ingredients

1 x 400g (14oz) can of
  chickpeas (garbanzo beans)
3 tablespoons tahini
1 garlic clove
1 large lemon
½ teaspoon ground cumin
2 tablespoons extra virgin olive
  oil, plus a little extra to serve
salt and black pepper
sprinkle of paprika (optional)

HOUMOUS

This is super easy to make and goes perfectly with the lamb koftas on page 42. It's also great for dipping carrots into!

1   Place a sieve over a bowl and tip in the chickpeas to drain them, saving the liquid. Put the chickpeas and tahini into a food processor. Peel the garlic clove and add this too. Cut the lemon in half and squeeze the juice into a small bowl, removing any pips (see page 14) . Add the cumin, olive oil, half the lemon juice and a pinch each of salt and pepper. Pop the lid on the food processor and blitz everything together.

2   Taste the houmous. If you think it needs more lemon juice or salt or pepper, add a bit more. If it's a little too thick, you can add a bit of the chickpea liquid.

3   Scoop it into a bowl, cover it with clingfilm and pop it in the refrigerator. When ready to serve, drizzle your houmous with a bit of olive oil and a sprinkle of paprika, if you like.

Ingredients

1 large ripe tomato
3 ripe avocados
1 garlic clove
handful of coriander
    (cilantro) sprigs
½ lime
2 pinches of chilli powder
¼ teaspoon salt
4 twists of black pepper
drizzle of olive oil

CHUNKY GUACAMOLE

I love avocados and this recipe is great alongside the Chicken Quesadillas on page 34, or on its own with a stack of tortilla chips when your mates come over. It's so easy to make you'll never bother buying it from the shop again!

1 Firstly, using a knife and being careful, chop your tomato into little chunks, then tip them into a medium bowl.

2 Scoop out your avocados (see page 13) straight into the bowl with the tomato. Mash them together with a fork.

3 Peel and crush the garlic (see page 13) and finely chop the coriander, saving a few whole leaves to serve.

4 Squeeze the lime juice into the avocados, and add the garlic, coriander, chilli powder, salt and pepper. Give it a good mix with the fork and taste it to check you're happy.

5 Spoon your guacamole into a serving bowl, drizzle with some olive oil and sprinkle with the reserved coriander leaves.

TIP: If you're not serving straight away, save one of the avocado stones and pop it in the guacamole, as it helps stop it from going brown. Cover with clingfilm and pop it in the refrigerator until you're ready to eat.

SERVES 6 – 8

Ingredients

2 x 400g (14oz) cans of
    chopped tomatoes
½ red onion
1 garlic clove
handful of coriander (cilantro)
1 teaspoon white wine vinegar
¼ teaspoon ground cumin
¼ teaspoon salt
¼ teaspoon sugar
½ lime

TOMATO SALSA

Another quick and easy recipe to add to your list! This goes perfectly with the Chicken Quesadillas on page 34.

1 Open the cans of tomatoes and tip the contents into a sieve placed over a sink or large bowl. Leave to drain.

2 Peel and finely chop the onion half and the garlic and roughly chop the coriander.

3 Put the drained tomatoes into a medium bowl and add the rest of the ingredients, squeezing in the lime juice. Give it a stir and refrigerate for at least 30 minutes before serving.

TIP: If you like your salsa less chunky, pop it into a food processor and give it a few pulses.

SWEET

Blueberries are so good for you and it makes sense to have them served in a muffin! These are soft, moist, fluffy muffins with a sparkling sugar crust. I love how quick and simple these are to make, and you only need one bowl, so hardly any washing up to do afterwards. These are great for parties or as a teatime treat!

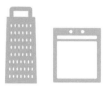

MAKES 9

Ingredients

70g (⅓ cup) unsalted butter
1 lemon
100g (½ cup) granulated sugar
175g (¾ cup) sour cream
1 large egg
½ teaspoon vanilla extract
1½ teaspoons baking powder
¼ teaspoon bicarbonate
   of soda (baking soda)
¼ teaspoon salt
150g (1¼ cups) blueberries, fresh
   or frozen (no need to defrost)
195g (1½ cups) plain (all-purpose)
   flour, plus an extra tablespoon
   for the blueberries
9 teaspoons sparkling sugar (use
   granulated or demerara if you
   don't have any sparkling)

1   Preheat your oven to 180°C/350°F/Gas mark 4. Pop 9 muffin paper cases into a 9-hole muffin tin.

2   Melt the butter in a small bowl in the microwave, or a small saucepan over a low heat.

3   Finely grate the zest from the lemon (see page 14). Put the melted butter, sugar, sour cream, egg, vanilla extract and lemon zest into a large mixing bowl. Beat with a hand-held electric whisk (or stand mixer) until you have a nice, smooth mixture.

4   Add the baking powder, bicarbonate of soda and salt to the large mixing bowl and beat again.

5   Put your blueberries in a small bowl and sprinkle over the extra tablespoon of flour. Give them a little shake to make sure they are all coated in the flour (this prevents them from sinking to the bottom of the muffins).

6   Using a sieve, sift the flour into the large mixing bowl. Add the flour-coated blueberries and gently mix with a wooden spoon. The batter will be quite thick, which is perfect.

7   Spoon the batter into the prepared muffin cases and then sprinkle each muffin with a teaspoon of sparkling sugar (or whichever sugar you are using).

8   Place the tin in the oven and bake for 25–30 minutes until the tops of the muffins are golden and a skewer or cocktail stick inserted into the middle of one of the muffins comes out clean. Let the muffins cool in the tin for 10 minutes, then carefully take them out of the tin in their cases and leave to cool completely on a wire rack. Once cool, you can devour!

VERY BERRY BLUEBERRY MUFFINS

APPLE ROSE TARTS

These little pastry tarts look beautiful and are simple to make. Perfect for Mother's Day, or in fact, any special occasion where you want to impress people with your baking skills! They may seem a little bit intimidating to make at first, but you'll get the hang of them in no time.

MAKES 8

———

Ingredients

15g (1 tablespoon) butter
4 red-skinned apples (Pink
    Lady or Royal Gala are lovely)
juice of ½ lemon
240ml (1 cup) apple juice
a few drops of red food colouring
1 x 375g (13¼oz) packet
    of pre-rolled all-butter
    puff pastry
plain (all-purpose) flour,
    for dusting
2 tablespoons apricot jam
3 tablespoons caster
    (superfine) sugar
2 tablespoons ground cinnamon
icing (confectioners') sugar,
    for dusting
cream or ice cream, to serve

1   Preheat your oven to 200°C/400°F/Gas mark 6. Melt the butter in a small bowl in the microwave, or in a small saucepan over a low heat. Dip a pastry brush into the melted butter and brush the insides of a 12-hole muffin tin.

2   Core the apples (see page 16) then cut them in half from top to bottom. Lie each apple half flat on a chopping board and cut each across into thin slices (not too thin or they will break up when heated). Place the apple slices into a large microwavable bowl or saucepan and add the lemon juice and apple juice. Top up with cold water until the apple is covered. Add the red food colouring and give it a gentle mix with a spoon. Microwave the apples for 4 minutes, or place over a medium heat, until they are bendy but not too soft. Once they are cooked, using tongs, take the apple slices out of the liquid and place them on kitchen paper to drain.

3   Place the pastry on a floured surface, keeping the longer length of the rectangle nearest you.

4   Warm the apricot jam with a splash of water in a small bowl in the microwave, or in a small saucepan over a low heat. Mix it with a teaspoon to make sure it is runny. Dip a pastry brush into the glaze and brush it all over your pastry, going all the way to the edges.

5   In a small bowl, mix together the caster sugar and cinnamon with a spoon, then use your fingers to sprinkle it evenly all over the apricot glaze. With a big knife, cut the pastry rectangle into strips from top to bottom, about 3–4cm (1¼–1½ inch) wide.

6   Place some apple slices along the first strip of pastry, peel side facing out, overlapping them slightly, then gently roll the strip up to make a tart (see photos). Place the tart in one of your prepared muffin cups. Repeat the process until you have made as many tarts as you can with your pastry.

7   Bake your cute little tarts in the oven for about 20–25 minutes until the pastry looks crisp, golden brown and puffed up. Be careful, as you don't want the apples to burn on the top – stay close to keep an eye on them!

8   Take the tarts out of the oven and leave them to cool for about 10 minutes, then gently lift each one out of the tin and onto a cooling rack. When cool, dust with icing sugar and serve with cream or ice cream.

BANANA PANCAKE PARCELS WITH MAPLE PECANS

This is a great recipe to learn for Pancake Day, or for any other day of the year! This dish is so yummy, but please take care when cooking it as you are working with very hot sugary syrup that can easily burn. If you have a nut allergy, just leave out the pecans. Oh, and if you fancy mixing up this recipe, try serving it with a scoop of ice cream and chocolate sauce too.

MAKES 8

———

Ingredients

For the pancakes
130g (1 cup) plain
   (all-purpose) flour
2 medium eggs
250ml (1 cup) milk
80ml (⅓ cup) water
unsalted butter, for frying

To assemble and serve
4 ripe bananas
30g (¼ cup) pecans (optional)
4 tablespoons maple syrup
pinch of sea salt
crème fraîche

1 Using a sieve, sift the flour into a large bowl, trying not to get it everywhere! Add the eggs and milk and whisk everything together. Add the water and whisk again until smooth. Now you have a batter.

2 Place a 20–22cm (8–8¾ inch) frying pan over a medium heat and add a knob of butter (or you could use cooking oil spray). Tilt the pan to spread the melted butter all over the surface. When the butter starts to bubble, use a ladle to pour some batter into the pan, tilting the pan again to swirl the batter all over the surface. Let the pancake cook for about 1 minute until it's a golden-brown colour underneath (give it a little shake – if it moves that's a good sign).

3 Now here's where you can have a bit of fun! Either toss your pancake without it hitting the ceiling (get a grown-up to show you how to do this!) or use a spatula to flip it over. Cook the other side of the pancake for 30 seconds and then slide it out of the pan on to a warm plate. Cover with some foil to keep the pancakes warm. Repeat this process until you have used up all the batter. You should be able to make 8 pancakes with the mixture, but it will depend on the size of your pan and how thick you like your pancakes.

4 Time to peel your bananas. After that, cut them into chunky pieces. Roughly chop the pecans, if using.

5   In a large frying pan (or use the same one that you used for the pancakes, to save on washing up!) melt at least 2–3 tablespoons of butter over a low heat until it starts bubbling. Add your bananas to the pan and fry for 2 minutes until golden brown. Carefully turn them over using a spatula. Add the pecans, if using, and cook everything for a few more minutes. If the pan is drying out, just add a little more butter.

6   Just to be safe, lower the heat a little, then add the maple syrup and a pinch of salt to the pan. Cook for a few moments longer then take the pan off the heat and let it cool slightly.

7   Grab yourself some serving plates. Place a pancake on one plate, spoon some caramelized banana mixture into the middle, then fold it into a triangle. Spoon more of the banana on top, add a dollop of crème fraîche then drizzle with some of the sticky syrup from the pan. Repeat with the other pancakes and enjoy!

My grandparents grew up not far from Bakewell, a small market town in Derbyshire, UK. Now, although there is no evidence that the cherry Bakewell originated from that town, I still want to dedicate this recipe to them! These cute little tarts remind me of my childhood, and when I make them I feel like I'm ten years old again. Some people use cherry jam for these, but I don't think it matters to be honest; just use whatever jam you have in the house, but make sure it has a high fruit content to balance out the sweetness of the icing.

This recipe uses a flaky crumbly pastry, raspberry jam and a frangipane – three things you can and will learn to make yourself from scratch. Once you have mastered these pastry skills, it will be a great foundation to go on to try more technical recipes. I have included a recipe for quick-fix jam, which is a simple way to make jam, rather than the more complicated version for setting and storing.

MAKES 12

———

Ingredients

15g (1 tablespoon) butter
4 tablespoons raspberry or
 strawberry jam (see page 89
 for homemade)
125g (generous ¾ cup) icing
 (confectioners') sugar
12 glacé cherries,
 or 6 cut in half

(ingredients continued
on the next page)

1   It's important to start by making your pastry so it has time to rest and chill – this makes it easier to roll out and prevents it shrinking during the baking process. Put the butter and sugar in a large bowl and cream together, using a wooden spoon, until light and fluffy. Add the egg yolks and mix again. Next add the flour and salt and mix very briefly to form a ball of dough. Knead it for a minute in the bowl with your hands until smooth. Wrap the dough in clingfilm and stick it in the refrigerator for half an hour.

2   Melt the 15g (1 tablespoon) of butter in small bowl in a microwave, or in a small saucepan over a low heat. Dip a pastry brush into the melted butter and brush the insides of a 12-hole muffin tin.

3   It's time for the frangipane. Cream the butter and sugar together in a large bowl just like you did for the pastry. Add the eggs, ground almonds, flour, baking powder and lemon zest and mix again. Cover the bowl with clingfilm and place it in the refrigerator.

4   When your pastry has chilled, tip it on to a floured work surface. Using a rolling pin, roll it out to about 2–3mm (¹⁄₁₆–⅛ inch) thick (see page 19). The pastry is delicate and can be fiddly to handle but don't worry, just take your time. Use a cookie cutter slightly bigger than the holes in the muffin tin to stamp out 12 rounds of pastry, placing each round in a muffin hole as you go along – use a spatula to help you lift your circles. You may have to roll out your pastry a

CHERRY BAKEWELL TARTLETS

For the pastry

90g (⅓ cup plus 1 teaspoon)
    unsalted butter, at room
    temperature, plus extra
    for greasing
65g (5 tablespoons) caster
    (superfine) sugar
3 egg yolks (see page 17 for
    separating eggs)
200g (1½ cups) plain (all-purpose)
    flour, plus extra for dusting
pinch of salt

For the frangipane

125g (½ cup plus 1 tablespoon)
    unsalted butter
125g (scant ⅔ cup) caster
    (superfine) sugar
2 eggs
125g (1¼ cups) ground almonds
50g (6 tablespoons) plain
    (all-purpose) flour
½ teaspoon baking powder
finely grated zest of ½ lemon
    (see page 14)

**Quick-fix raspberry
or strawberry jam**

500g (1lb 2oz) raspberries or
    chopped-up strawberries
70g (6 tablespoons) caster
    (superfine) sugar
juice of 1 lemon

Place berries, sugar and lemon
juice in a medium saucepan.
Stirring with a wooden spoon, heat
until the contents come to a boil.
Turn the heat to low and cook
until the liquid has reduced and
your jam is thick. I don't mind the
seeds, but it can be quite annoying
getting them stuck in your teeth
so, once the jam has cooled down,
squish it through a fine sieve into a
bowl using the back of a spoon.

few times to make enough circles. If the pastry breaks just
patch it up and squish it in to make it fit in nicely. Once you
have filled the 12 muffin holes, place the tray back in the
refrigerator for 15 minutes to chill. Preheat your oven to
180°C/350°F/Gas mark 4.

5   Now it's time to blind bake the pastry. This is to make sure
    the pastry gets cooked at the bottom before the filling goes
    in. Pop small pieces of baking parchment into the chilled
    pastry cases and fill with baking beans or uncooked rice.

    TIP: To save time, I use cupcake cases instead of baking
    parchment – just scrunch them up and unroll them before
    adding to the pastry cases and pouring in the baking beans!

6   Place the pastry cases in the oven to bake for 10 minutes,
    then take them out and remove the beans or rice and paper
    (be careful as everything will be hot – or get a grown-up to
    help you).

7   Fill each pastry case with a teaspoon of jam and then a
    tablespoon of frangipane. Don't over-fill: it takes practice
    to know how much mixture you need to put in – the first
    time I made these the mixture overflowed! Bake the tartlets
    in the oven for 15–20 minutes or until the pastry is nicely
    golden, then remove them from the oven and leave to cool
    in the tin. When they are completely cool, carefully lift them
    out of the tin.

8   For the topping, mix the icing sugar with a teaspoon of water
    in a medium bowl. Keep adding water, in teaspoon amounts,
    until you get a thick but spoonable icing. Spoon the icing
    into the middle of the tartlets, pushing it to the edges with
    the back of the spoon, then place a cherry on top of each
    (I cut mine in half). Leave the icing to set before serving.

CLASSIC VICTORIA SPONGE

This is a British classic, to my mind. It's an easy sponge to make, using equal amounts of the main ingredients – a great recipe for your first layer cake, because it's so simple.

SERVES 8–12

Ingredients

250g (1 cup plus 2 tablespoons) unsalted butter, at room temperature, plus extra for greasing
250g (1¼ cups) caster (superfine) sugar
4 large eggs
1 teaspoon vanilla extract
250g (1¾ cups plus 2 tablespoons) self-raising flour
2 teaspoons baking powder
2 tablespoons milk
150ml (10 tablespoons) double (heavy) cream
5–6 tablespoons raspberry or strawberry jam (see page 89 for homemade)
1 teaspoon icing (confectioners') sugar, for dusting

1   To make your sponges, you will need two 20cm (8 inch) round, loose-bottomed cake tins or a non-stick springform cake tin. Spread some butter round the inside of the tins with your fingers, then put baking parchment on the bases of the tins (draw a circle on the parchment around the base of the tin, then cut it out with scissors). Preheat your oven to 180°C/350°F/Gas mark 4.

2   In a large mixing bowl, beat together the butter and sugar using a hand-held electric whisk (or stand mixer) until light and fluffy. Add the eggs one at a time, beating between each egg, then add the vanilla extract and mix again.

3   Using a sieve, sift the flour and baking powder into the large mixing bowl, then gently fold everything together with a wooden spoon. Add the milk and fold gently once more.

4   Using a big spoon, divide the mixture evenly between the two tins. Level the tops with the back of the spoon.

5   Bake the sponges in the oven for about 25 minutes (every oven is different so have a peek after 20 minutes and stay close by!). You want your sponges to have risen, be lightly golden brown and be soft and springy when touched on the top (don't burn your fingers). Stick a skewer or cocktail stick into the middle of your sponges; if it comes out clean, they're ready.

6   Remove from the oven and leave the sponges to cool in the tins for 10 minutes. Run a blunt knife around the edge of each cake (just inside the tin) to ensure they haven't stuck. Remove the cakes from the tins by pushing up the base from the sides. The cakes will still be warm and this is a bit fiddly, so be careful or get a grown-up to help you. Remove the bases of the tins and peel the baking parchment off the bottom of the sponges. Place them on a wire rack, bottom side down, and leave to cool completely.

7   Put the cream in a large, clean bowl and, using a hand-held electric whisk (or stand mixer), whip until just thick enough to spread, taking care not to over-whip it; it should still be spoonable. Choose the sponge with the best-looking top and turn the other sponge upside down and place on a flat serving plate.

8   Spread the jam over the sponge with a spoon, then spread the whipped cream on top of the jam. Place the other sponge on top and use a sieve to dust a teaspoon of icing sugar over the cake. You are now ready to serve!

I clearly remember eating lots of watermelon when I visited America many years ago, and it tasted so good. Now I love eating anything that tastes of watermelon, including these little gems which I enjoy making with the family. It takes a bit of patience, as you have to wait while each layer sets, so you might plan to make them the day before you want to eat them.

MAKES 8

———

Ingredients

600g (1lb 5oz) chunk
  of watermelon
½ lemon
3½ tablespoons granulated
  sugar, plus more to taste
  if needed
a few drops of red food
  colouring
120ml (½ cup) canned coconut
  milk (give the can a good
  shake before opening)
4 apples
60ml (¼ cup) water
a few drops of green food
  colouring

You will need ice lolly
moulds that allow you to
add your own sticks

1   Ask a grown-up to cut a watermelon in half for you, then use an ice-cream scoop to scoop the flesh out of the watermelon, flicking out the black seeds as you go. Squeeze the lemon half into a small bowl to give you 1 tablespoon of juice. Put the watermelon into a blender with 2 tablespoons of the sugar, the lemon juice and a few drops of red food colouring. Blend until smooth, then give it a taste and, if it needs to be a little sweeter, add a bit more sugar – but hopefully the watermelon will be sweet enough. Using a spoon, skim off any foam, then pour the juice into a jug. Pour the juice into each lolly mould to about two-thirds full, trying not to splash the sides (you need a steady hand!). Cover with the lid and insert the lolly sticks. Pop in the freezer for 3 hours.

2   It's time for our next layer. In a medium bowl, whisk the coconut milk with the remaining 1½ tablespoons sugar until the sugar has completely dissolved. If the mixture is too thick (you need a pourable consistency), just thin it out with a tablespoon of water. Pour the coconut mixture into a jug and place it in the refrigerator until you're ready.

3   After 3 hours, grab your ice lollies, remove the mould lid and carefully pour a thin layer of coconut milk over the watermelon layer. Return to the freezer, uncovered, for at least an hour.

4   Right, time for the third and final layer! Peel your apples and remove the cores (see page 16) then cut them into quarters. Put the apples in a blender with the water and blend until the apples are smooth. Next, place a sieve over a medium-sized bowl and pop in a piece of kitchen paper. Pour the apple juice into the lined sieve and let the juice drip through the sieve into the bowl below (this is to allow the pure juice to separate from any pulp).

ICY
WATERMELON
LOLLIES

5   Pour the apple juice into a jug and add some green food colouring until it reaches a colour you like. Pull your ice lollies out of the freezer and carefully pour your green apple mixture over the coconut milk. Return to the freezer for another few hours.

6   To remove your icy watermelon lollies from their moulds, place the sides of your lolly moulds under a warm tap (don't let the water touch the apple top), then slowly pull the sticks to slide the lollies from the moulds. You are ready to enjoy!

NOTE: You don't have to use food colouring if you don't want to – I just like that it makes the colour brighter!

NUTELLA CUPCAKE CHEESECAKES

If you're a fan of chocolate, then this is for you! I love the rich taste of Oreo biscuits, then added to that a creamy Nutella filling topped with whipped cream and finished off with chopped hazelnuts and grated chocolate. If you want to make a special treat for your mum or dad, stick a Ferrero Rocher on top!

MAKES 9

Ingredients

12 Oreo biscuits (cookies)
45g (3 tablespoons) unsalted butter
250g (generous 1 cup) cream cheese
30g (3½ tablespoons) icing (confectioners') sugar
½ teaspoon vanilla extract
240g (1 cup) Nutella
70ml (4½ tablespoons) double (heavy) cream

For the topping
180ml (¾ cup) double (heavy) cream
2 tablespoons icing (confectioners') sugar
handful of hazelnuts, finely chopped (optional)
chocolate, finely grated (optional)

1   Right, let's get going. Place your biscuits in a small plastic bag and bash them gently with a rolling pin until they turn into little crumbs. Make sure you don't tie the bag, trapping in air, as the bag will burst when you start crushing the biscuits, and the crumbs will go everywhere! Put the crushed biscuits in a medium bowl.

2   Melt the butter in a small bowl in the microwave, or in a small saucepan over a low heat, then add to the biscuit crumbs and stir with a wooden spoon until well mixed.

3   Place 9 muffin cases in a 9-hole muffin tin and divide your biscuit mixture between them with a spoon. Press the mixture down with the back of the spoon to make a base, then put the tin in the refrigerator to chill and set.

4   Time to make your cheesecake filling. Put the cream cheese into a medium bowl and mix using hand-held electric beaters (or stand mixer) until smooth. Add the icing sugar and vanilla extract and mix again until you have a nice, smooth mixture. Add the Nutella to the bowl and mix again, then add the cream and mix again until the cheesecake filling is completely smooth.

5   Take the muffin tin out of the refrigerator, then spoon your cheesecake filling evenly on top of the biscuit bases and smooth the tops with the back of the spoon. Pop the tin back in the refrigerator and chill the cheesecakes for at least 5 hours or, for best results, overnight.

6   Lift the cheesecakes out of the tin. In a medium bowl, whisk the cream and icing sugar together with a hand-held electric whisk until thick. Spoon a dollop of cream on top of each of the cheesecakes. Decorate with chopped hazelnuts or grated chocolate, or both. Delicious!

If you're wanting a cute, bite-sized dessert, well, these are for you. I think they taste like mini apple pies. Plus, you can have some fun with the can of whipped cream!

MAKES 20–25

Ingredients

5 large flour tortillas
60g (4 tablespoons)
   unsalted butter
150g (¾ cup) granulated sugar
2 teaspoons ground cinnamon
4 Granny Smith apples
1 tablespoon freshly squeezed
   lemon juice
1 teaspoon grated nutmeg
small can of whipped cream

1   Preheat your oven to 200°C/400°F/Gas mark 6 and grab yourself a 12-hole muffin tin.

2   Next, you need to cut 4–5 circles from each tortilla, using an 8cm (3¼ inch) cookie cutter. Put the circles on a plate (and eat the scraps!). Melt the butter in a small bowl in the microwave, or a small saucepan over a low heat. Spoon 2 tablespoons of the melted butter into a little bowl for later.

3   Put the remaining half of the melted butter in a large bowl with 50g (¼ cup) of the sugar and 1 teaspoon of the cinnamon. Give it a mix with a spoon. Add the cut-out tortilla circles to the bowl and make sure they are all coated with the mixture.

4   Turn the muffin tin upside down and place as many of the tortilla circles in between the muffin cups as you can – they should be folded in half into a taco shape – then bake in the oven for 5–6 minutes, until crisp and turning golden. Take the tortillas out of the oven and carefully remove them from the tin with tongs. Repeat with more tortilla circles until all of them are cooked.

5   Now to make a start on the apples. Carefully peel and core your apples (see page 16) and chop them into small pieces (they have to fit into your tacos). Pop the apples into a medium saucepan with the lemon juice, the remaining 100g (½ cup) sugar, the remaining 1 teaspoon of cinnamon, the nutmeg and the leftover melted butter. Cook over a medium heat for about 10 minutes, stirring with a wooden spoon, until the apples are soft. Remove from the heat and leave to cool. Taste the apple mixture to make sure that you're happy with the flavours, adding more lemon juice, sugar or cinnamon if you like.

6   Using a teaspoon, spoon your cooled apple mixture into the crisp taco shells. It's a bit fiddly, so just take your time. Top them with a squirt of whipped cream, trying not to get it everywhere!

SPICED APPLE TACOS

STRAWBERRY
AND LIME
POTS

This is a quick and delicious dessert you can make to impress your parents and friends. I love the flavour combination of lime and strawberry, but if you want, you can leave out the lime jelly and simply make some mousses. See what you think and use your imagination for decorating your delicious creations.

MAKES 4

Ingredients

1 x 135g (4¾oz) packet of lime
   jelly (jello)
200g (7oz) strawberries, hulled
   (stalks and stems taken out),
   plus an extra 4 to serve
2 tablespoons granulated sugar,
   plus extra if needed
60g (¼ cup) full-fat
   cream cheese
½ teaspoon vanilla extract
180ml (¾ cup) double (heavy)
   cream, chilled
2 tablespoons caster
   (superfine) sugar

1 Carefully read the instructions on your jelly packet and make it in a jug. Grab four glasses and pour equal amounts of jelly into each one, to about half way up. Put them in the refrigerator to set for at least a couple of hours before making the mousse.

2 To make the mousse, put the strawberries and granulated sugar in a food processor and whiz them until smooth. At this point, give it a taste to check if you're happy with the sweetness, adding a little bit more sugar if necessary. Add the cream cheese and vanilla extract and whiz again for a few more seconds.

3 Pour the cream into a large bowl and add the caster sugar. Using a balloon whisk (or hand-held electric whisk on a low speed), whisk the cream and sugar until the mixture begins to thicken slightly. It should still be soft so be careful not to over-whisk – it will firm up more as it chills later. Pour the strawberry mixture into the whipped cream and gently whisk them together until everything is mixed.

4 With a teaspoon, spoon the mousse over the set jelly until you reach the top of the glass. Cover each glass with clingfilm and pop them back into the refrigerator to set for at least an hour.

5 When you're ready to serve, decorate each with a strawberry.

If you ask your parents about rock buns they'll probably reminisce about how they learned to make them at school in Home Economics – the name for a cooking class many years ago. My gran used to make them all the time. I liked them because they were dry, not too sweet and looked like... well, rocks. We called my gran 'Mama' and she was a cook in the Caribbean, so she would make hers with a bit of extra spice and coconut. Here's my version of her Jamaican rock buns.

MAKES 12

Ingredients

75g (½ cup) raisins
225g (1¾ cups) self-
    raising flour
2 teaspoons baking powder
⅛ teaspoon salt
½ teaspoon grated nutmeg
½ teaspoon ground mixed spice
100g (½ cup minus 1
    tablespoon) unsalted butter,
    at room temperature
75g (⅓ cup) demerara
    (brown) sugar
40g (½ cup) desiccated
    (dried shredded) coconut
1 egg
4 tablespoons milk
1 teaspoon vanilla extract
granulated sugar, for sprinkling

1   Put the raisins into a small bowl, cover them with warm water, then put the bowl aside to let the raisins soak.

2   Preheat the oven to 200°C/400°F/Gas mark 6. Pop a piece of baking parchment on a large baking tray.

3   Put the flour, baking powder, salt and spices in a large mixing bowl. Cut the butter into small cubes, then add it to the flour mixture. With your fingertips, rub the butter into the flour until the mixture looks like tiny little breadcrumbs. (Don't give up if your fingers start aching!)

4   Tip the raisins into a sieve over the sink to drain. Add the raisins, demerara sugar and desiccated coconut to the flour mixture. Then mix everything together with a wooden spoon.

5   Crack the egg into a jug or medium bowl (see page 17), add the milk and vanilla extract and mix everything together with a fork. Tip this into the mixing bowl with the dry ingredients and, using a wooden spoon or spatula, mix everything together until it forms a light, airy dough. Don't over-mix – stop stirring when everything is just combined.

6   Using a tablespoon, blob the mixture onto your baking sheet, spaced well apart, to form 12 rough mounds. If your baking tray isn't large enough, that's fine, you can bake in two batches. Sprinkle the rock buns with granulated sugar.

7   Bake the rock buns in the oven for 12–15 minutes, until golden brown. Take them out of the oven and leave to cool for 10 minutes on the baking tray, before placing the rock buns on a wire rack to cool completely. These are best eaten the same day, but I don't mind them a bit crumbly a day later! I also freeze mine.

JAMAICAN
ROCK
BUNS

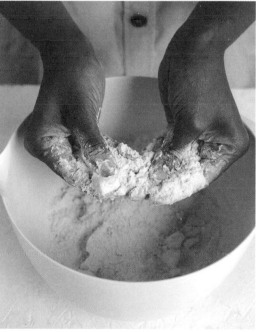

MONSTER
CRISPY
TREATS

You won't believe how easy it is to rustle up these little monsters and they look awesome. They are so yummy, having both a delicious sweet marshmallow flavour as well as a crispy texture. But be warned, this is a sticky affair! You will need to use the stove for one part of the recipe, so if you're not yet at the stage to cook over a stove, just get an adult to help with that bit and you can finish off. The monster decoration adds to the fun and makes these great for Halloween or even a party, but they are just as good served plain – whatever takes your fancy!

**MAKES
12 LARGE OR
16 SMALL**

Ingredients

40g (3 tablespoons) unsalted
   butter, plus extra for greasing
150g (6 cups) puffed rice cereal
⅛ teaspoon salt
285g (7 cups) miniature white
   marshmallows
½ teaspoon vanilla extract
90g (½ cup) of each colour of
   candy melts you want to use
1 teaspoon vegetable oil for each
   candy melt colour, plus extra
   if needed
edible candy eyes
   (or chocolate chips)

1   First things first, you need to grease your equipment. Melt a large knob of butter in a small bowl in the microwave, or in a small saucepan over a low heat. Dip a pastry brush into the melted butter and brush it all over a 23cm (9 inch) square baking tin, a medium saucepan, a spatula and also a large mixing bowl (one that will comfortably hold all your cereal). This is to stop everything sticking!

2   Pour the puffed rice cereal into the greased mixing bowl.

3   Put the 40g (3 tablespoons) butter and the salt in the greased saucepan over a medium–low heat. Add the marshmallows and stir constantly with your greased spatula until the marshmallows have completely melted.

4   Add the vanilla extract to the pan and mix again. Pour the mixture over the cereal in the mixing bowl and stir with the spatula until the cereal is coated in the marshmallow gloop.

5   Pour the mixture into the greased baking tin and, with the greased spatula, gently press it down until you have a flat surface. Put the tin into the refrigerator until the mixture is firm. When it is completely cold, use a knife to cut the mixture (still in the tin) into 12 or 16 rectangles. Remove the treats from the tin.

6   For the monster coating, put one colour of candy melts in a small bowl and melt in the microwave for 1 minute. Stir with a small spoon and then microwave again for 30 seconds at a time until completely melted. Repeat with the other colours.

7   Add the oil to the melted candy melts and stir until it is completely mixed in. Add a little more oil to make the melts smoother if you need to, but only add it a little bit at a time.

8 Holding a treat by one end, carefully dip it into the candy melt mixture, then place it on a cooling rack or plate. Gently press some candy eyes or chocolate drops into the candy melt icing – make your monster look however you want!

9 Continue making more little monsters with the same colour, or repeat steps 6–8 for each different candy melt colour you'd like to use.

10 Be patient and wait at least 45 minutes, until your monster crispy treats have hardened, before eating them!

This cake is delicious because it has the perfect balance – it's neither too sweet nor too tangy. The best part is you get to decorate it with lemon drop sweets – one of my favourites when I was little. I've now convinced myself to cut down on eating them, to stop the roof of my mouth from getting sore!

SERVES 8

———

Ingredients

2 lemons
175g (¾ cup plus 1 teaspoon)
   unsalted butter, plus extra
   for greasing
175g (¾ cup plus 2
   tablespoons) caster
   (superfine) sugar
3 large eggs
125g (1 cup minus 1 tablespoon)
   self-raising flour
50g (½ cup) ground almonds
1 teaspoon baking powder

For the icing
1 lemon
200g (scant 1½ cups) icing
   (confectioners') sugar
a few lemon drop sweets

1   Preheat your oven to 180°C/350°F/Gas mark 4. Finely grate the zest of both lemons. Cut one of the zested lemons in half with a sharp knife and squeeze out the juice into a small bowl, picking out any pips (see page 14).

2   Melt a knob of butter in a small bowl in the microwave, or in a small saucepan over a low heat. Dip a pastry brush in the melted buter and brush it all over a 450g (1lb) loaf tin, then pop in a big piece of baking parchment that extends above the sides of the tin (this will help to lift the cake out of the tin when cooked).

3   In a large mixing bowl and using a hand-held electric whisk (or stand mixer), beat together the butter, sugar and lemon zest until it is light and fluffy. It will start to produce a wonderful lemony smell.

4   Add the eggs to the mixing bowl one at a time, beating between each egg, then add the lemon juice and beat again for a few seconds.

5   Using a sieve, sift the flour into the mixing bowl, then add the ground almonds and baking powder. Gently beat the mixture again to make sure all the ingredients are mixed together well.

6   Using a big spoon to help scrape, tip your cake mixture into your loaf tin and bake in the middle of your oven for 40–45 minutes. Check if the cake is ready by inserting a skewer or cocktail stick into the centre – if it comes out clean it's ready. Remove from the oven, put it on a wire rack, and leave to cool in the tin for 10 minutes.

LEMON
DROP DRIZZLE
LOAF

7   Using the overhanging baking parchment, carefully lift the cake out of the tin. If it's sticking to the sides, use a blunt knife to go around the edges of the tin to loosen it. Place the cake on the wire rack to cool completely.

8   To make your lemon icing, zest half the lemon (see page 14), and finely grate the rest. Cut the zested lemon in half and squeeze the juice into a medium bowl, removing any pips. Using a sieve, sift the icing sugar into the bowl, add the finely grated zest and stir with a spoon until you have a smooth paste. With the spoon, drizzle the icing evenly all over the top of your cake.

9   Crush the lemon drops by lightly bashing them with a rolling pin on a chopping board (still in their wrappers), then remove all the wrappers and sprinkle the crushed drops over the top of the cake, along with the remaining lemon zest. Place on a serving plate and slice!

MINI
FRUIT
PAVLOVAS

Years ago, I used to be afraid of making meringue – I was a bit silly, I admit! I want you all to feel confident about making it sooner rather than later because, to be honest, it's not difficult and tastes better when made at home. If you're not happy with the results first time, do not give up! Just try again and soon you will be producing elaborate meringues like they do on all the baking shows. You'll have egg yolks left over from making these, but don't throw them away. There are loads of things you can make with them (custard, mayonnaise, ice cream...) including the pastry for the Cherry Bakewell Tartlets on page 86.

SERVES 6

Ingredients

For the meringue
4 large egg whites (see page 17 for separating eggs)
pinch of salt
250g (2¼ cups) caster (superfine) sugar
1 teaspoon cornflour (cornstarch)
1 teaspoon white wine vinegar
½ teaspoon vanilla extract

For the filling
250ml (1 cup) double (heavy) cream
250g (generous 1 cup) mascarpone, at room temperature
1 teaspoon vanilla extract
30g (3½ tablespoons) icing (confectioners') sugar, plus extra for dusting
mixture of fresh berries, or any fruit you love!
mint leaves (optional)

1 Preheat your oven to 160°C/320°F/Gas mark 3. Pop a piece of baking parchment on to a large baking tray and draw 6 circles about 10cm (4 inches) wide on the parchment with a pencil, leaving space in between the circles. (If your oven has two shelves, prepare another baking tray just in case you have extra meringue.)

2 Pour your egg whites and a pinch of salt into a large, clean bowl and whisk with a hand-held electric whisk (or stand mixer) until the egg whites hold firm peaks.

TIP: Tilt the bowl slightly – if the eggs stay put and don't slip down the side of the bowl they are at firm peaks and ready for the sugar.

3 Gradually add the sugar, one spoonful at a time, whisking all the time until you have a bowl of glossy, snowy meringue.

4 Pop the cornflour, vinegar and vanilla in a small cup and mix with a teaspoon until smooth, then whisk it into the meringue mixture with the electric hand-held beaters. You'll be pleased to know the hard bit is now done!

5 Grab your baking tray and take the baking parchment off. Get a teaspoon and put a tiny dollop of the meringue on each corner of the baking tray to stick the parchment to the tray. Place the baking parchment back on the tray, with the circle markings on the underside (you will still be able to see them). Fill the circles with meringue mixture; use a tablespoon to do this, spreading and smoothing it out within the lines of your circles. You need to make sure you also create a dip in the centre of each meringue, with the back of the spoon, so that the cream and fruit have somewhere to sit (the first time I tried making this, I didn't follow this instruction and all my toppings fell off!).

6   Slide your baking tray into the oven, then immediately turn it down to 140°C/275°F/Gas mark 1 and bake for 30 minutes. Turn the oven off and let your meringues cool in the oven for an hour. Take them out of the oven and put them on to a wire rack to cool completely. Be careful because they are very delicate.

7   When you are nearly ready to serve, put the cream, mascarpone, vanilla and icing sugar into a medium bowl and whip with a hand-held electric whisk (or stand mixer) until it is soft and fluffy. Give it a taste: if you want it a little bit sweeter, add a bit more icing sugar, if it's too sweet, add a drop more cream and mix again.

8   Use a teaspoon to dollop the cream into the dips of your meringues and smooth it down. Place some fruit on top of the cream and then use a sieve to dust over a teaspoon of icing sugar. If you want to be really flash, add a little piece of mint! *Bon appétit!*

I remember being at primary school fêtes, walking past the stalls and seeing a huge array of wonderful cakes and never having enough pocket money to buy all the ones I wanted. It was the butterfly cakes that always caught my eye. They looked delicious and light, and I wanted them to flutter straight into my mouth. Maybe you could make these for your school cake sale and create some memories for someone else too!

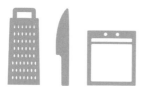

MAKES 12

Ingredients

1 orange
110g (½ cup minus 1 teaspoon)
  unsalted butter, at room
  temperature
110g (½ cup plus 1 tablespoon)
  caster (superfine) sugar
2 large eggs
175g (1⅓ cups) self-raising flour
1 tablespoon milk
sprinkles (optional)

For the buttercream
1 orange
115g (½ cup) unsalted butter,
  at room temperature
230g (2 cups) icing
  (confectioners') sugar,
  plus extra for dusting
2 tablespoons milk, if needed

1   Preheat the oven to 190°C/375°F/Gas mark 5. Pop 12 cupcake paper cases into a 12-hole cupcake tin.

2   Finely grate the zest from the orange and squeeze out the juice (see page 14). Measure out 2 tablespoons of the juice into a small bowl (you can drink any left over!).

3   In a large bowl, beat the butter and sugar together with a hand-held electric whisk (or stand mixer) until light and fluffy. Add the eggs and beat again, then add the flour, orange zest, the 2 tablespoons juice and the milk, and keep beating until you have a smooth cake mixture.

4   Using a tablespoon, spoon an equal amount of the mixture into each of the paper cases and bake in the centre of the oven for 15–20 minutes. Keep an eye on the cakes and check them after 15 minutes. When they are ready, the cakes should be risen and golden. Take them out of the oven and leave to cool for 10 minutes in the tin, then carefully take them out of the tin and put them on a wire rack to cool completely.

5   Time to make your orange buttercream. Finely grate enough zest from the orange to give you ½ teaspoon, then cut the orange in half and squeeze the juice into a small bowl. Measure out 2 tablespoons of juice. Put the orange zest and juice, butter and icing sugar into a medium bowl and, using the electric hand-held whisk, mix until you have a smooth paste. If you need to loosen it, add the milk a little at a time.

6   To turn your cakes into butterflies, you will need a small, sharp knife and a steady hand. Be careful here or ask for help. You need to angle your knife into the middle of your cakes to allow you to cut out a cone-shaped piece of sponge, leaving a little hole in the middle (see photos). Cut the cone-shaped pieces of cake in half to make the wings of your butterflies.

ORANGE BUTTERFLY CAKES

7 Use a teaspoon to fill the holes of your cakes with buttercream. Add two butterfly wings to each cake on top of the buttercream and press them down very gently. Put your butterfly cakes on a serving plate.

8 Using a sieve, dust a teaspoon of icing sugar over your cakes, then add some sprinkles, if you like.

I think this is a fantastic way to make your five-a-day a little bit more colourful. There's no technical ability needed for this, just a good eye for presentation to help you enjoy some delicious fruit. If you're not usually a fan of fruit, maybe this will change your mind! This recipe is easy to rustle up, so give it a go.

MAKES 10

———

Ingredients

20 blueberries
10 red grapes
10 green grapes
4 kiwi fruit, peeled and cut
    into 10 chunks
10 chunks of pineapple
2 mangoes, peeled and cut
    into 10 chunks
2 tangerines or mandarins
    (seedless if possible),
    separated into segments
    (you need 10)
10 strawberries
10 raspberries

For the honey yogurt dip
240ml (1 cup) Greek yogurt
2 tablespoons honey
½ teaspoon vanilla extract

You will need 10
wooden skewers

1   Put the yogurt, honey and vanilla extract into a small bowl and mix together with a spoon. Give it a taste and add more honey or vanilla if you like, then place it in the refrigerator.

2   Take one of your wooden skewers and then thread on 2 blueberries, 1 red grape then a green one, a chunk of kiwi, pineapple, mango, tangerine, a strawberry and then finally a raspberry. Repeat this until you have 10 made-up skewers or you have used up all your fruit.

3   Place the fruit skewers on a large plate fanned out in a rainbow shape. When ready to serve, take the honey dip out of the refrigerator and enjoy!

RAINBOW
SKEWERS

INDEX

THANK YOUS!

We can see you Charlie! Props were proper!

Harry, the loveliest and best editor in the world. Fact.

Silver Fox Ellis who took all the pictures

Tamara, just as lovely as her food styling!

My sous chef Michael. Couldn't have done it without you!

Me. Obvs.

Sarah! The big boss. Just as crazy as her hair!

Luke, designer extraordinaire. You rock!

Plus, I need to thank my bosses who I also count as friends: Sandy Smith and Carla-Maria Lawson at the BBC, and all the team over at *MasterChef* because this book wouldn't have happened without you.

Anna-Louise Naylor, you are a gem for connecting me to Sarah at Quadrille and thank you for all the help and advice you gave me. Speaking of which, there needs to be a 'BIG UP' for everyone over at Quadrille Publishing who have been an absolute dream – thank you for being so welcoming, as I didn't have a clue about the book world before this! Then there's the one and only Mr Hugill – Glenn, you are a 'G', my Ambassador of Quan, and you know why. Oh, and then all my food testers, ranging from the doctor's surgery to the car garage, with a special mention to my neighbours, especially Ella, Ben, Chloe and Max. Also I can't forget all of the lovely children photographed in the book – you are all stars. And finally, my husband Michael and gorgeous little ones, who helped crack eggs, made extra mess for me whilst I was trying to cook, had the recipes for dinner more than once, and always washed up whilst I was busy in the kitchen. You guys are the best and I love you to the moon and back.